MW01243573

Mason Jar Meals

Super Quick and Easy Mason Jar Meals for Busy People Who Value Health

By Ashley Strong

Published in Canada

© Copyright 2015 – Ashley Strong

ISBN-13: 978-1508654407
ISBN-10: 1508654409

Table of Contents

Introduction

I want to thank you and congratulate you for choosing this book, *"Mason Jar Meals"*.

Are you tired of having to order take out or eat out because you never seem to have enough time to prepare home cooked meals? Are you tired of having to waste a lot of money on buying food? Do you want to always come home to a nice meal? Do you also want to be able to easily carry around your lunch?

Well if this is you, then this book is just perfect for you. This book discusses in detail the concept of preparing meals in jars. You will learn how to prepare different recipes in jars and important information on how to adequately pack foods to ensure that the meals last long while still maintaining their flavor.

Thanks again for choosing this book, I hope you enjoy it!

Chapter 1:
Mason Jar Meals
Why the Craze

Recently people have begun preparing meals in jars, and for good reasons. In current society, lives are always hectic and every second, minute, hour, and day counts. Therefore, we never have time to do important things such as preparing home cooked meals. This is why most people have turned to eating out, ordering take out, or even eating junk foods like fries, pastries and other not-so-healthy food options.

This is why the rates of obesity and obesity related illnesses are on the rise. The good thing is that more people are seeing how their poor eating habits are harming them and are consequently trying to find healthier options. However, time is the greatest limiter for most people. This is how the concept of Mason jar meals came about. With Mason jar meals, one can simply prepare the food in advance and have enough food for the week. Mason jar meals last longer than other stored foods, even up to five days, since you can ensure that the jar is airtight. Additionally, they are easier to carry around than food in lunch box which may spill easily. As long as you close the lid tightly, you will not have to worry about your sauces messing up your bag.

Most people are also afraid of carrying salads to work since the vegetables can become soggy from the dressing. However, with the proper arrangement of ingredients in the jar, you can ensure that the veggies remain crunchy. Before you can start preparing your Mason jar meals, it is critical to understand generally how to arrange the ingredients in the jars.

The Best Jars to Use and How to Layer Food in the Jars

The best jars for preparing Mason jar meals are those with a wide-mouth as it is much easier to arrange the layers in. Pint-sized jars are suitable for packing smaller meals, while quart-sized jars are most suitable for larger meals.

The greatest challenge for many people when preparing meals in jars is layering ingredients. If you do not properly pack the foods, they will become soggy. For example, whenever packing salads in Mason jars, you have to start with the dressing at the bottom. From there, you add the heavier, non-absorbent ingredients followed lastly the lighter ingredients, which in most cases will be salad greens. With the other meals, the trick is simply to ensure that the heavier ingredients are at the bottom and the lighter ingredients are at the top.

Now that you understand the concept of layering your food well, let us get started in preparing Mason jar meals.

Chapter 2:
Breakfast in a Jar

Vanilla & Oats Breakfast in a Jar

Serves: 3

Ingredients

2 tablespoons pumpkin seeds

½ cup rolled oats

1 cup almond milk

1 cup vanilla yogurt

2 tablespoons coconut, toasted and shredded

1 cup cherries

Directions

Combine pumpkin seeds, rolled oats, milk and yogurt in a bowl and mix until well combined. Divide ingredients between 2 (8 ounce) jars. Top with coconut and cherries.

Maple Syrup with Banana in a Jar

Serves: 2

Ingredients

1 cup unsweetened almond milk

½ cup oats

2 tablespoons chia seeds

2 teaspoons cinnamon

½ teaspoon vanilla

2 tablespoons peanut butter

1 banana, sliced

2 tablespoons pecans, chopped

2 teaspoons maple syrup

Directions

Combine almond milk, chia seeds, oats, cinnamon, and vanilla in a bowl, and mix until well combined. Cover and let sit for at least 8 hours. Place the peanut butter and bananas in a small microwave safe bowl. Microwave for about 20 seconds until peanut butter is melted. Add oat mixture to the peanut butter mixture, and mix until well combined. Divide the ingredients between the 2 (8-ounce) jars. Top with pecans and maple syrup.

Cereal Breakfast Mix in a Jar

Serves: 4

Ingredients

4 cups rolled oats

3 tablespoons chia seeds

2 teaspoons ground cinnamon

3 tablespoons flax seeds

½ tablespoon salt

1 cup vanilla whey protein powder

1 cup dried fruits

1 cup wheat germ

1 cup oat bran

Directions

Combine all the ingredients in 4 (1-pint) jars.

Mango Breakfast Smoothie in a Jar

Serves: 2

Ingredients

1 mango, cubed

¾ cup unsweetened coconut milk

1 cup nonfat plain Greek yogurt

2 tablespoons honey

1 banana

1 tablespoon chia seeds

½ teaspoon vanilla extract

¼ teaspoon ground allspice

1 cup ice cubes

Directions

Combine all of the ingredients in a blender, and blend until smooth. Divide smoothie mixture between 2 (12-ounce) jars. Cover and refrigerate for 1 hour.

Baked Egg in a Jar

Serves: 4

Ingredients

4 eggs

½ cup milk

2 tablespoons scallions, chopped

1 pound diced ham

¼ cup mozzarella cheese, shredded

Pepper to your preference

Salt to taste

Directions

Preheat oven to 350 degrees Fahrenheit. Spray the 4 jars with cooking spray. Combine eggs and milk in a bowl and mix until well blended. Add scallions to the egg mixture and stir well. Season with pepper, and salt to taste. Divide the egg mixture between 4 (8-ounce) jars. Top each jar mixture with the ham and cheese. Bake for 25 to 30 minutes, or until golden brown.

Baked Tomatoes with Eggs in a Jar

Serves: 2

Ingredients

4 Roma tomatoes, halved and seeded

4 eggs

½ teaspoon salt

1 tablespoon red pepper flakes

2 tablespoons fresh cilantro, chopped

Directions

Preheat oven to 450 degrees Fahrenheit. Divide the tomato halves between 2 (8-ounce) jars. Crack 2 eggs in each jar on top of the tomatoes and season with salt and red pepper flakes. Bake for 6-7 minutes. Remove from oven. Top with herbs the cover with lid.

Peanut Butter and Yogurt Smoothie in a Jar

Serves: 2

Ingredients

1 banana

4 tablespoons peanut butter

1 cup chocolate almond milk

4 tablespoons yogurt (preferably Greek yogurt)

2 teaspoons honey

2 tablespoons cocoa powder

Directions

Combine all ingredients in a blender, and blend until smooth. Divide the smoothie mixture between 2 (8-ounce) jars. Cover and refrigerate for at least 1 hour.

French Toast in a Jar

Serves: 6

Ingredients

1 loaf (450g) French bread, cut into 1-inch cubes

8 eggs, lightly beaten

4 teaspoons sugar

3 cups milk

2 tablespoons butter

1 teaspoon vanilla extract

¾ teaspoon salt

2 teaspoons ground cinnamon

Directions

Preheat oven to 350 degrees Fahrenheit. Spray 6 (1-pint) jars with cooking spray. Combine all of the ingredients in a large bowl, and mix until well combined. Divide the mixture between the 6 jars. Bake for 45-50 minutes or until a knife inserted in the center of a jar comes out clean.

Berry Parfait with Vanilla Ricotta and Toasted Almonds

Serves: 6

Ingredients

4 cups fresh berries (e.g. blueberries, raspberries, or black berries)

1 tablespoon granulated sugar

2 tablespoons chopped basil

1/3 cup almonds, sliced

1 tablespoon and 1 teaspoon fresh lemon juice

For Vanilla bean Ricotta

Zest of ½ lemon

½ teaspoon honey

2 tablespoons granulated sugar,

1 vanilla bean, seeded

1 ½ cups fresh, skim ricotta

Directions

Combine the basil, berries, lemon juice, and sugar in a bowl. Cover and refrigerate for twenty minutes in order to allow the berries to juice.In a sauté pan over medium heat, toast the sliced almonds for approximately three minutes.

Place all of the ingredients for the vanilla bean ricotta in a large bowl, and mix using a hand mixer on medium until smooth.To assemble the Mason jar, spoon 2 ½ tablespoons of the vanilla bean ricotta mixture into each (8-ounce) jar. Top the first layer with toasted almonds and ½ cup of the berry mixture. Repeat this arrangement a second time, and top with the remaining almonds.

Serve immediately or refrigerate until ready to eat within 3 days.

Chapter 3:
Salads in a Jar

Brown Rice & Nori Sheet Salad in a Jar

Serves: 4

Ingredients

1 tablespoon soy sauce

1 tablespoon rice vinegar

1 teaspoon sugar

2 cups white or brown rice (cooked)

2 cups nori sheets (16 sheets), cut into small pieces

2 avocados, seeds removed, diced

1 cucumber, peeled and cut into small pieces

1 cup lump crab meat

2 tablespoons lemon juice

Directions

In a small saucepan, heat soy sauce, vinegar and sugar over medium heat until the sugar is dissolved. Add rice and toss to combine. Remove from the heat and let sit for a few minutes at room temperature.

In four (1-pint) jars, layer ½ cup of the rice mixture followed by ½ cup of the chopped nori sheets. Top with ½ cup avocado, ½ cup cucumber, and finally ¼ cup crab meat. Sprinkle each salad mixture with lemon juice.

Beats & Beans Salad in a Jar

Serves: 4

Ingredients

¼ cup olive oil

¼ cup apple cider vinegar

2 teaspoons honey

1 tablespoon Dijon mustard

Ground black pepper

Salt to taste

2 beets, shredded

1 cup garbanzo beans, rinsed and dried

1 cup baby spinach, lightly packed

1 large carrot, shredded

Directions

Combine the apple cider vinegar, olive oil, honey and Dijon mustard in a bowl, and mix until well combined. Season with pepper and salt to taste. Layer ¼ cup beets then add ¼ cup beans followed by ¼ cup spinach and lastly ¼ cup carrots in each of the 4 (8-ounce) jars. Pour the dressing over the mixture within each jar.

Artichokes with Lemon Salad in a Jar

Serves: 2

Ingredients

One 14-ounce can quartered artichoke hearts, drained

1 tablespoon lemon juice

2 garlic cloves, sliced

1 teaspoon Italian seasoning

2 tablespoons olive oil

1 teaspoon salt

1 teaspoon black pepper

1 tablespoon oregano

Directions

Divide the quartered artichoke hearts, lemon juice, garlic, Italian seasoning, olive oil, salt, and black pepper between 2 (8-ounce) jars. Top with oregano.

Tomato Salad in a Jar

Serves: 2

Ingredients

3 red plum tomatoes, diced

1 bunch fresh basil leaves, chopped

3 orange plum tomatoes, diced

3 yellow plum tomatoes, diced

1 cup baby spinach, loosely packed

8 tablespoons balsamic vinaigrette

2 cups orzo pasta, cooked

2 tablespoons olive oil

1 tablespoon lemon juice

Ground black pepper

Salt to taste

Directions

First layer with ½ of the red tomatoes then ½ of the basil leaves followed by ½ of the orange tomatoes, ½ of the yellow tomatoes, ½ cup baby spinach, 4 tablespoons balsamic vinaigrette and 1 cup 0rzo pasta in each of 2 (1-quart) jars. Combine olive oil and lemon juice in a bowl, and mix well. Season the oil lemon mixture with salt and pepper and pour over each salad.

Berries Salad in a Jar

Serves: 4

Ingredients

2 tablespoons olive oil

2 tablespoons lemon juice

1 tablespoon lemon zest

¼ cup orange juice

1 tablespoon honey

2 cups blackberries

2 cups strawberries, sliced

2 cups blueberries

1 cup roasted almonds, chopped

Directions

Combine olive oil, lemon juice, lemon zest, orange juice, and honey in a bowl. Mix until well combined. Layer ½ cup blackberries, ½ cup strawberries and ½ cup blueberries in each of the 4 (1-pint) jars. Top each jar mixture with almonds and pour the dressing over each salad.

Taco Salad in a Jar

Serves: 4

Ingredients

6 tomatoes, chopped

2 cups corn

1/2 head romaine lettuce, chopped

2 cups black beans

1 pound ground turkey meat

2 medium scallions, chopped

8 tablespoons fresh salsa

2 cups cheddar cheese, shredded

Directions

Divide the ingredients into four and in each jar, layer with tomatoes, then corn, lettuce, black beans, turkey meat, scallions and 2 tablespoons fresh salsa in each of the 4 (pint-size) jars. Top with cheese.

Spring Salad in a Jar

Serves: 4

Ingredients

¼ cup orange juice

2 tablespoons olive oil

2 tablespoons lemon juice

Ground black pepper

Salt to taste

1 cucumber, chopped

6 tomatoes, chopped

2 cups peas

1 medium bunch of radishes, chopped

1/2 head romaine lettuce, chopped

1 cup crumbled feta cheese

Directions

Combine orange juice, olive oil, and lemon juice in a bowl. Mix until well combined and season with salt and pepper. Divide the other ingredients into four then start layering the ingredients starting with cucumber, followed by tomatoes, then peas, radishes and finally lettuce in each of 4 (1 pint) jars. Top with cheese. Pour the dressing over each salad jar.

Egg Salad in a Jar

Serves: 4

Ingredients

2 tablespoons olive oil

2 tablespoons lemon juice

3 tablespoons apple cider vinegar

Ground black pepper

Salt to taste

6 eggs, hard boiled and chopped

6 tomatoes, chopped

2 avocadoes, chopped

2 cups baby spinach, chopped (loosely packed)

Directions

Combine olive oil, lemon juice, and apple cider vinegar in a bowl and mix until well combined. Season with salt and pepper. Divide the other ingredients into four then start layering starting with hardboiled eggs, then tomatoes, avocado, and finally spinach in each of the 4 (1 pint) jars. Pour the olive oil mixture over each salad.

Prawn and Tomato Salsa Salad

Serves: 1

Ingredients

5 raw king Prawns, peeled and deveined

1 teaspoon coconut oil

½ teaspoon salt

½ teaspoon cumin powder

½ teaspoon sweet paprika

½ teaspoon red chilli flakes

2 garlic cloves, diced finely

Tomato Salsa

2 diced tomatoes

¼ red onion, diced finely

2 tablespoons chopped coriander

¼ lime

½ avocado diced

½ teaspoon salt

1 head chopped iceberg lettuce, tightly packed

2 tablespoons extra virgin olive oil

Juice of ½ lime

Additional coriander for garnish

Directions

Heat coconut oil in a large pan then toss the prawns with spices, garlic and sea salt. Fry the prawns for 3-4 minutes, stirring frequently to ensure even cooking. Once cooked, set aside to cool before packing your salad.Combine the salsa ingredients in a large bowl, and put at the bottom of a (1-pint) jar, followed by the prawns, lettuce, avocado, lime, and extra coriander on top.

Chapter 4:
Savory Meals in a Jar

Lasagna in a Jar
Serves: 6
Ingredients
1 pound ricotta
1 egg
¼ cup Parmesan cheese
3 cups marinara sauce
12 ounces wide egg noodles, cooked
½ teaspoon salt
2 cups mozzarella cheese
Directions
Preheat oven to 350 degrees Fahrenheit. Spray 6 (12-ounce) jars with cooking spray. Combine ricotta, egg, parmesan, marinara sauce, noodles, salt and mozzarella in a bowl and mix until well combined. Divide the mixture between the 6 jars. Bake for 30 to 35 minutes until golden brown.

Pumpkin & Macaroni in a Jar

Serves: 6

Ingredients

2 tablespoons butter, melted

1 cup milk

¼ teaspoon nutmeg

1 cup whipped cream

2 tablespoons all-purpose flour

½ teaspoon of salt

2 cups pumpkin, cubed

¼ teaspoon black pepper

2 cups elbow macaroni, cooked

1 cup Fontina cheese

Directions

Preheat the oven to 350 degrees Fahrenheit. Melt butter in a pan, add milk, nutmeg, and whipped cream. Bring to a boil. Add flour, salt and pepper and cook for 5 minutes on medium heat until it thickens. Remove from the heat. Add pumpkin and macaroni and mix well. Divide between 6 pint-sized jars. Top with cheese. Bake for 30 to 35 minutes Serve immediately or refrigerate and eat within 3 days.

Noodle Soup in a Jar

Serves: 1

Ingredients

1 cup rice noodle sticks

¼ bouillon cube

1 cup carrot, shredded

½ cup cabbage, shredded

½ cup chopped baby spinach, loosely packed chopped

1/8 teaspoon garlic powder

¼ teaspoon ginger, grated

1 ½ cups boiling water

1 tablespoon soy sauce

½ teaspoon lime juice

Ground black pepper

Salt to taste

Directions

Combine noodles, stock cube, carrots, cabbage, spinach, garlic powder, and ginger powder in a (1 quart) jar. Pour boiling water over the mixture. Cover and let sit for 10 to 12 minutes until noodles are soft and stock cube is dissolved. Add soy sauce and lime juice, and mix well. Season with salt and pepper.

Vegetables & Shrimp in a Jar

Serves: 2

Ingredients

½ medium avocado, mashed

1 tablespoon apple cider vinegar

½ small onion, chopped

¼ head lettuce, shredded

½ lb tomatoes, chopped

¼ cup parsley, chopped

2 teaspoons fresh jalapeno, chopped

2 tablespoons ketchup

1 tablespoon lime juice

1 pound shrimp, cooked and cut in pieces

½ cup tortilla chips, coarsely crumbled

Directions

Combine mashed avocados and vinegar in a bowl and mix well. Set aside. Combine onion, parsley, tomatoes, jalapeno, lettuce, ketchup, lime juice, and shrimp in another bowl, and mix until well combined. Season with salt and pepper. Spread the avocado mixture in the bottom of 2 (1- quart) jars. Layer ½ cup shrimp mixture in each jar. Top with tortilla chips and close the jar.

Chicken Stew in a Jar

Serves: 6

Ingredients

1 tablespoon olive oil

1 pound chicken breast, cut into small cubes

4 cups water

4 carrots, sliced

8 potatoes, sliced

2 onions, chopped

¼ cup parsley, chopped

2 tablespoons basil

¼ cup unbleached flour

1 teaspoon salt

½ teaspoon pepper

Directions

Preheat the oven to 350 degrees Fahrenheit. In a medium pot, heat oil on medium heat. Add chicken and cook for 5 minutes. Add water, carrots, potatoes, onions, parsley and basil and mix well. Bring to a boil. Add flour, salt and pepper and mix well. Remove from the heat. Divide the mixture between 6 (10-ounce) jars and bake for 25 to 30 minutes until done.

Wild Rice in a Jar

Serves: 4

Ingredients

2 tablespoons red wine vinegar

1 tablespoon lemon juice

1 teaspoon sugar

1/3 cup olive oil

¼ teaspoon salt

½ teaspoon ground pepper

1 cup cooked wild rice

½ red onion, chopped

1 clove garlic, minced

½ cup dried cranberries

½ scallion, chopped

½ celery stalk, chopped

1/3 cup pecans, toasted and chopped

1/3 cup cashews, toasted and chopped

Directions

Combine vinegar, lemon juice, sugar, oil, salt, and pepper and set aside. Combine rice, onion, garlic, cranberries, scallions, celery, pecans, and cashew in a bowl, and mix well. Divide the rice mixture between 4 (6-ounce) jars and pour the vinegar mixture over each salad.

Black Lentils with Rice in a Jar

Serves: 4

Ingredients

2 tablespoons olive oil

5 curry leaves

1 teaspoon cumin seeds

¼ teaspoon mustard seeds

2 tablespoons black lentils

¼ cup water

1 teaspoon turmeric

3 green chilies, chopped

4 cups cooked brown rice

Salt to season

¼ cup parsley, chopped

Directions

In a large pan, heat oil on medium heat. Add curry leaves, cumin seeds and mustard seeds, and fry for 20 seconds. Add black lentils and water and cook for 10 minutes until thickened. Add turmeric and green chilies and cook for 1 minute. Add rice and salt and mix until well combined. Remove the mixture from heat. Divide the mixture between 4 (12-ounce) jars. Top with parsley.

Lentil Soup in a Jar

Serves: 4

Ingredients

3 tablespoons butter

1 clove of garlic, chopped

2 bay leaves

1 dried Chile pepper

2 teaspoons turmeric

1 ½ teaspoons curry powder

½ teaspoon salt

5 sun-dried tomatoes

½ cup red lentils

½ cup yellow lentils

6 cups water

4 tablespoons coriander

Directions

In a pot, heat oil on medium heat, add garlic and cook for 1 minute until golden brown. Add bay leaves, Chile pepper, turmeric, curry powder, tomatoes, red lentil, yellow lentil and salt and mix well. Cover with water and cook for 10 to 15 minutes. Remove from the heat. Divide the mixture between 4 (16-ounce) jars. Top with coriander.

Chapter 5:
Quick Snacks in a Jar

Chocolate Chip Snack in a Jar

Serves: 3

Ingredients

1 cup dark chocolate chips

8 ounces black M&Ms

8 ounces white chocolate covered pretzels

5 ounces yogurt covered raisins

Directions

Combine all of the ingredients, and mix well. Divide the mixture between 3 (12-ounce) jars.

Vanilla Wafer in a Jar

Serves: 4

Ingredients

2 cups vanilla wafers, crushed

1 cup white baking chips

2 cups banana chips

1 cup almonds, chopped

Directions

Combine all of the ingredients and mix well. Divide the mixture between 4 (12-ounce) jars.

Berries in a Jar

Serves: 4

Ingredients

2 cups mixed berries

1 cup dark chocolate covered almonds

1 cup white chocolate chips

Directions

Combine all of the ingredients, and mix well. Divide the mixture between 4 (8-ounce) jars.

Popcorn in a Jar

Serves: 10

Ingredients

1 cup light corn syrup

1 cup honey

2 cups sugar

2 cups creamy peanut butter

1 teaspoon vanilla extract

2 cups popcorn, popped

3 cups cashews

Directions

In a nonstick pan, heat corn syrup and honey on medium heat. Add sugar and cook for 2 to 3 minutes until sugar has dissolved. Add peanut butter and cook for 2 minutes. Add vanilla extract and stir constantly until smooth. Remove from the heat. Add popcorn and cashews and toss to coat. Allow to cool and transfer to 10 pint-sized jars.

Puff Corn Snack in a Jar

Serves: 4

Ingredients

1 tablespoon butter flavored shortening

4 tablespoons white almond bark chocolate

1 cup white chocolate chips

2 cups puff corn

½ cup sprinkles

Directions

Melt butter-flavored shortening, chocolate and white chocolate chips in double boiler until smooth. Remove from the heat. Add puff corn and sprinkles, and toss to coat. Leave sit for a few minutes until set. Divide the mixture between 4 (6-ounce) jars.

Baked Banana in a Jar

Serves: 2

Ingredients

4 raw bananas, sliced

¼ teaspoon salt

¼ teaspoon pepper

Oil for frying

Directions

Combine bananas, salt and pepper in a bowl and mix well. In a pan, heat oil on medium heat. Add bananas and fry for 15 minutes until golden brown. Drain with paper towel. Allow to cool. Divide the mixture between 2 (4-ounce) jars.

Pinto Beans Snack in a Jar

Serves: 4

Ingredients

1 cup salsa-style refried pinto beans

1 cup guacamole

1 cup sour cream

1 cup fresh chunky salsa

1 cup black olives, sliced

1 cup cherry tomatoes, chopped

1 cup shredded cheddar cheese

1 large scallion, thinly sliced

Directions

Spread ¼ cup pinto beans along the bottom of 4 (12-ounce) jars. Layer ¼ cup guacamole, ¼ cup sour cream then ¼ cup chunky salsa followed by ¼ cup olives, ¼ cup tomatoes, and ¼ cup cheese. Top with scallions.

Quick Pineapple Snack in a Jar

Serves: 6

Ingredients

2 cups pineapple chunks

1 cup cherries

1 cup cool whip

2 cups mandarin orange segments, drained

1 cup coconut, shredded

Directions

Combine pineapple, cherries, cool whip, and mandarin orange segments in a bowl, and mix well. Divide the mixture among 6 (8-ounce) jars. Top with coconut.

Pasta Snack in a Jar

Serves: 1

Ingredients

1/3 cup pasta, uncooked

½ cup water

1/4 cup milk

½ cup cheddar cheese, shredded

Directions

Combine water and pasta in an 8-ounce jar. Microwave the jar for 4 to 5 minutes until the pasta is cooked. Remove from microwave and stir. Add milk and cheese and mix well. Microwave for 1 minute until cheese is melted. Eat immediately from the jar or seal and refrigerate to eat later.

Cranberries in a Jar

Serves: 10

Ingredients

3 cups cranberries

½ cup orange juice

¼ cup brown sugar

1 ¼ cups granulated sugar

2 teaspoons ginger

1 cup apple, peeled and chopped

1 cup raisins

Directions

In a large pan, add orange juice, brown sugar, and granulated sugar, and mix well. Cook on medium heat for 5 minutes until sugar dissolves. Add cranberries, ginger, apple, and raisins, and cook for another 5 minutes. Keep stirring until thickened. Remove from the heat. Divide the mixture between 10 (4-ounce) jars.

Cinnamon Roll in Jar

Serves: 1

Ingredients

For Cream Cheese Icing

2 tablespoons cream cheese, softened

2 teaspoons milk

4 tablespoons powdered sugar

For the Cinnamon Roll

4 tablespoons applesauce

2 tablespoons oil

2 tablespoons buttermilk

½ cup all-purpose flour

½ teaspoon of vanilla extract

4 tablespoons brown sugar

½ teaspoon baking powder

½ teaspoon ground cinnamon

1/8 teaspoon salt

Directions

Combine cream cheese, milk and powdered sugar in a bowl and mix until well combined, then set aside. Combine applesauce, oil, buttermilk, flour, brown sugar, cinnamon, vanilla extract, baking powder and salt in a bowl and mix until well combined and smooth. Put the mixture in 12-ounce jar. Microwave the jar on high for 1 minute and 15 seconds. Top with cream cheese icing.

Chocolate Pudding in a Jar

Serves: 4

Ingredients

1 ¾ cups 1nstant chocolate pudding mix (package)

2 cups milk

2 cups heavy cream

1 teaspoon vanilla

4 tablespoons graham cracker crumbs

1 cup marshmallow fluff

Directions

Combine instant chocolate pudding mix, milk, and vanilla in a pan and mix until well blended. Cook on medium heat for 5 minutes until smooth. Remove from heat and let sit for 5 minutes. Add heavy cream and stir until well mixed. Allow to cool thoroughly. Next, layer 1 tablespoon of graham cracker crumbs in each of 4 (12-ounce) jars. Cover cracker crumbs with 1 cup of the cooled pudding mix in each jar. Top with marshmallow fluff. Microwave for 1 minute until the marshmallow fluff is browned.

Panna Cotta in a Jar

Serves: 6

Ingredients

1 ¼ cups buttermilk

2 ¼ teaspoons gelatin

½ cup sugar

1 ½ cups whipping cream

½ cup blueberries

Directions

Combine buttermilk and gelatin in a pan and mix well. Cook the mixture on medium heat for 2 minutes. Add sugar and cook for another 3 minutes, until sugar dissolves. Remove from the heat, and add whipping cream. Mix until well combined. Divide the mixture between 6 (4-ounce) jars, top with blueberries, and place in the refrigerator for 1 hour until it sets.

Orange Cupcake in a Jar

Serves: 24

Ingredients

1 box yellow cake mix

3 eggs

½ cup orange juice

½ cup water

3 drops orange food coloring

1 teaspoon orange zest

For orange frosting

2 tablespoons butter, softened

2 cups powdered sugar

2 tablespoons half-and-half

1 teaspoon orange zest

½ teaspoon vanilla extract

Directions

Preheat oven to 350 degrees Fahrenheit. Combine all of the cake ingredients in a bowl, and mix until well blended. Divide the cake mixture between 24 four-ounce jars, filling the jars only half way. Bake for 20 to 25 minutes. Once cooked through, remove the cupcakes from the oven, and allow to cool.

To make orange frosting combine all of the orange frosting ingredients in a mixing bowl, and beat until well combined. Top the cupcakes with the orange frosting.

Baked Vanilla & Chocolate Fudge in a Jar

Serves: 4

Ingredients

2 eggs, beaten

2 tablespoons cocoa powder

½ cup butter, melted

2 tablespoons all purpose flour

1 cup white granulated sugar

1 teaspoon brown sugar

1 teaspoon vanilla extract

1 teaspoon chocolate extract

Directions

Preheat oven to 325 degrees Fahrenheit. Combine the eggs and sugars in a mixing bowl until well combined. Then add incocoa powder, butter, all purpose flour, vanilla extract and chocolate extract beat until well blended, don't overmix. Divide the mixture between 4 (4-ounce) jars and bake for 40 to 50 minutes until crisp.

Brownie in a Jar

Serves: 2

Ingredients

4 tablespoons butter, softened

2 tablespoons brown sugar

4 tablespoons white sugar

Pinch of salt

½ teaspoon vanilla extract

2 egg yolks

8 tablespoons plain flour

2 tablespoons cocoa powder

4 tablespoons chocolate chunks

3 tablespoons water

Directions

Combine butter, brown sugar, white sugar, salt, vanilla extract and egg yolks in a bowl. Add flour and cocoa powder, and mix well until well combined. Fold in chocolate chunks, and divide the mixture between 2 (12-ounce) jars. Place the jars in the microwave and cook for 1 minute.

Crunchy Cookie in a Jar

Serves: 2

Ingredients

2 tablespoons butter, melted

2 tablespoons brown sugar

2 tablespoons white sugar

½ teaspoon vanilla extract

2 egg yolks

Pinch of salt

2 tablespoons water

6 tablespoons plain flour

3 tablespoons corn flakes

3 tablespoons oatmeal

Directions

Combine the butter, salt, vanilla and the sugars first and mix until well blended. Then add the egg yolks and mix until you cannot see any egg yolk. Fold in the flour, oatmeal and the cornflakes until well blended. Divide the mixture between 2 (4-ounce) jars. Place the jars in the microwave, and cook for 2 minutes.

Banana Cream Pie in a jar

Serves: 4

Ingredients

3 sliced bananas

1 sheet of puff pastry, thawed

1 Vanilla pudding mixture (below)

Vanilla Pudding

2 teaspoons vanilla extract

1 egg

½ cup heavy cream¼ cup sugar

1/8 teaspoon salt

3 tablespoons of cornstarch

1 cup of unsweetened almond milk

¾ cup fat free milk

Directions

Place puff pastry on a clean surface and cut into 24 equal pieces. Transfer this pastry to a baking sheet, and bake until golden brown. Let the puff pastry cool thoroughly.

To make the vanilla pudding, heat the almond milk, heavy cream, and milk in a pan over medium heat until it simmers. Whisk together, sugar, salt, egg and cornstarch in a bowl. Remove milk mixture from heat, and slowly pour it into the cornstarch mixture, whisking constantly. Return the mixture to the pan over medium heat and whisk until the mixture thickens.

Remove pudding from the heat, transfer to a bowl, wrap bowl with plastic wrap, and let it cool before placing in the refrigerator to chill.

To assemble the banana pie, begin by placing two pieces of puff pastry into each of the 4 sixteen-ounce jars. Add the vanilla pudding, a few banana slices, and two more pieces of pastry. Top the layers with a banana slice. You can eat immediately or cover with plastic wrap and eat later. It can last up to 5 days.

Chapter 6:
Beverages in a Jar

Fruit Tea in a Jar

Serves: 1

Ingredients

½ cup lemonade, prepared

½ cup fruit tea, prepared

2 lemon slices

Directions

Combine the lemonade and fruit tea in an 8-ounce jar. Add lemon slices, and mix well.

Cold Coffee in a Jar

Serves: 1
Ingredients
½ cup cold coffee
1 tablespoon chocolate syrup
½ cup almond milk, unsweetened
3 ice cubes
Directions
Combine the cold coffee, chocolate syrup, and almond milk in an 8-ounce jar, and mix well. Add ice cubes and serve immediately.

Ginger Ale Shirley in a Jar

Serves: 1*Ingredients*
½ cup ginger ale
½ cup orange juice
2 tablespoons grenadine
½ cup lime soda
½ cup crushed ice
2 lime slices
Directions
Combine ginger ale, orange juice, grenadine, lime soda, and ice in a 12-ounce jar and mix well. Top with lime slices.

Watermelon Drink in a Jar

Serves: 1

Ingredients

1 cup watermelon, cubed

½ cup lime soda

½ cup ice, crushed

1 teaspoon mint leaves

Directions

Combine all of the ingredients in blender, and blend until smooth. Transfer the mixture to an 8-ounce jar and top with mint leaves.

Peach & Coconut in a Jar

Serves: 1

Ingredients

1 tablespoon peach nectar

½ cup coconut milk

½ cup apple juice

1 banana, sliced

½ cup ice, crushed

1 peach, sliced

Directions

Combine peach nectar, coconut milk, apple juice, banana, and ice in a blender, and blend until smooth. Transfer the mixture to an 8-ounce jar. Top with peach slices.

Pineapple & Mango Colada in a Jar

Serves: 2

Ingredients

1/3 cup cream of coconut

1/3 cup light rum

½ cup pineapple juice

1 medium mango, cubed

2 tablespoons lime juice

1 cup ice, crushed

Directions

Combine all of the ingredients in a blender, and blend until smooth. Transfer the mixture to 2 (8-ounce) jars.

Kiwi Soda in a Jar

Serves: 4

Ingredients

1 can lemonade concentrate, thawed

3 cups carbonated lemon-lime beverage

4 kiwi fruits, peeled

1 cup ice, crushed

Directions

Combine all of the ingredients in a blender and blend until smooth. Divide the mixture between 4 (8-ounce) jars.

Raspberry Vodka in a Jar

Serves: 2

Ingredients

1 cup raspberry vodka

2 raspberries

2 tablespoons lime juice

1 cup cranberry juice

1 cup ice, crushed

2 lime slices

Directions

Combine raspberry vodka, raspberries, lime juice, cranberry juice, and ice in a blender, and blend until smooth. Divide the mixture between 2 (8-ounce) jars, and top with lime slices.

Sweet Tea Lemonade

Serves: 8

Ingredients

8 black tea bags

3 cups sugar

4 large sprigs mint

1 lemon sliced

1 cup fresh lemon juice

10 cups water

Instructions

Mix 3 cups of water and sugar in a pan over medium heat and bring to a boil, stirring constantly until the sugar dissolves. Turn off the heat and stir the mint and lemon slices in. Allow the mixture to cool, then strain.

Bring 4 cups of water to a boil. Place the tea bags in a bowl and pour the boiling water over them to steep for approximately ten minutes. Then remove and discard the bags. Allow the tea to cool, and mix 3 cups of water with lemon juice.

Combine the lemon mixture, tea and syrup. Divide this final mixture between 8 (8-ounce) jars. Cover and chill for approximately 4 hours. Garnish with additional sprigs and lemon slices.

Conclusion

Thank you again for choosing this book!

I hope this book was able to help you to understand how to prepare Mason jar meals. The next step is to start preparing and enjoying a healthy meal every day. With Mason jar meals, you will not need to order take-out or eat out.

Finally, if you enjoyed this book, please post a review on Amazon.